100 Essential Steps

to

Less Stress & Anxiety

ISBN-10: 1-4196-9006-X
ISBN-13: 978-1-419-69006-8
Visit www.booksurge.com to order additional copies

Perfectionism produces anxiety;
learn to accept everything does not have to be perfect

A relaxing bath can restore tranquility

Learn to be aware of how you are breathing, rapid shallow breathing will worsen anxiety and cause hyperventilation

Self hypnosis and relaxation tapes can help retrain your
subconscious to become less anxious

When you are feeling anxious, call a friend, talk about how they are doing to distract your mind from how you are currently feeling

Try meditation to relax and quiet your mind

In difficult moments visualize a favorite place
and imagine yourself there

The mind can make things better or worse than they really are

Understand panic disorder is brought on by you and your own thoughts, control your thoughts and you will control your panic

Feel fear, let it pass, refocus on something positive

Clear clutter out of your bedroom,
the room needs to feel relaxing in order for you to sleep well,
not surrounded by things to be done

If you start to feel like you are about to have a panic attack
ask yourself if you are breathing slowly and deeply,
then refocus on controlling your breath

Take up yoga to learn how to relax and breathe deeply

Don't punish yourself for past mistakes,
you cannot change your past but you can shape your future

Aerobic exercise will help get rid of built up adrenaline
caused by being in an anxious state

Eliminate caffeine from your diet when you are feeling anxious

Drink chamomile tea to relax you

If you are driving and feel anxious,
find some music you like to sing along to and sing

Identify and stop anxiety producing self-talk

If you start to feel anxious,
splash your face and wrists with cold water

Be aware of when you are rushing and slow down

Keep a pad and pen in your bedside drawer to write down any thoughts circling your mind and preventing you from sleeping

Do not rely solely on others for your happiness,
you are responsible for your happiness

Appreciate the things that make your life valuable

Medications may give relief from anxiety
but they will not address the root of the problem

Force yourself to do what you are afraid of,
the sense of achievement will boost your self-confidence

A smile brightens the darkest day

Strength of the body is limited,
strength of the mind is not

Replace fears with a positive attitude and inner strength

When you feel happy, don't look too far ahead

Time is life; don't waste it focusing on stress and anxiety

Don't get so caught up in yourself that you forget to help others

Learn to say "no" when you feel under pressure

Learning to manage your time more effectively
can reduce stress

Every new day is a chance to invest in life

Open your eyes and appreciate the beauty of every day

Have enough reasons to want to stay healthy

Don't accommodate anxiety by restricting normal activities

Every big change starts with a small step

Busy people don't have time to worry,
keep your mind occupied

Be strong, be determined

Optimism is a great healing force

Spray lavender mist on your pillow before sleeping
to relax you

Listen to soothing classical music

Don't over analyze things

Try counseling if you need someone to talk
your problems through with you

Make peace with your past

Let go of disappointments of the past

Straighten out your problems before going to bed

Worry gives a small thing a big shadow

Don't worry what people think of you

Don't try to live up to someone else's expectations

If you find yourself hyperventilating, hold your breath for a minute and then focus on continuing to breathe slowly

Anxiety cannot harm you and will go away

When feeling anxious, don't add fear to fear
with negative self- talk

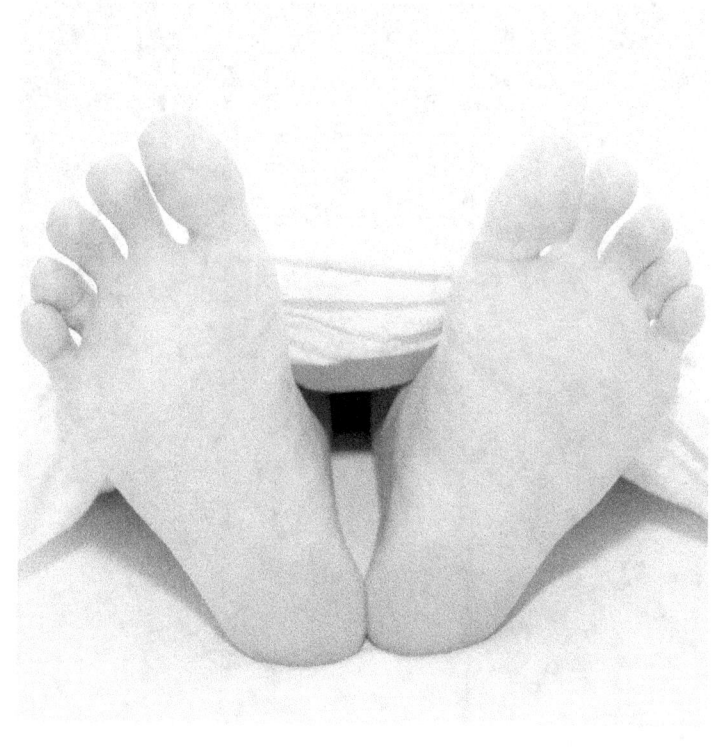

Try progressive muscle relaxation before sleeping; focus on relaxing each individual muscle in your body from head to toe

Restructure negative thoughts into rational responses

Life is what your thoughts make it

Get a massage to relive your body of tension

Aromatherapy can reduce stress, lavender is especially relaxing

Always have something to wish for

Keep a cheerful disposition,
it will make you and all those around you happier

Only you can help yourself

You can get through anything, you already have

Never trade tomorrow for a yesterday

Put all your energy into living in the present moment

Don't turn aggression inwards

Walking benefits physical and mental health

Do some gardening,
being amongst nature can lift your mood and create calm

Watching fish swim in an aquarium can be relaxing

When anxiety causes sensations in your body, remember,
they are just sensations and they will go away

Anticipation is usually greater than realization

Nicotine is a stimulant that can increase anxiety,
try to stop smoking

Failure isn't falling down, it's staying down

Read a cheerful or inspiring book

Places can be inspirational

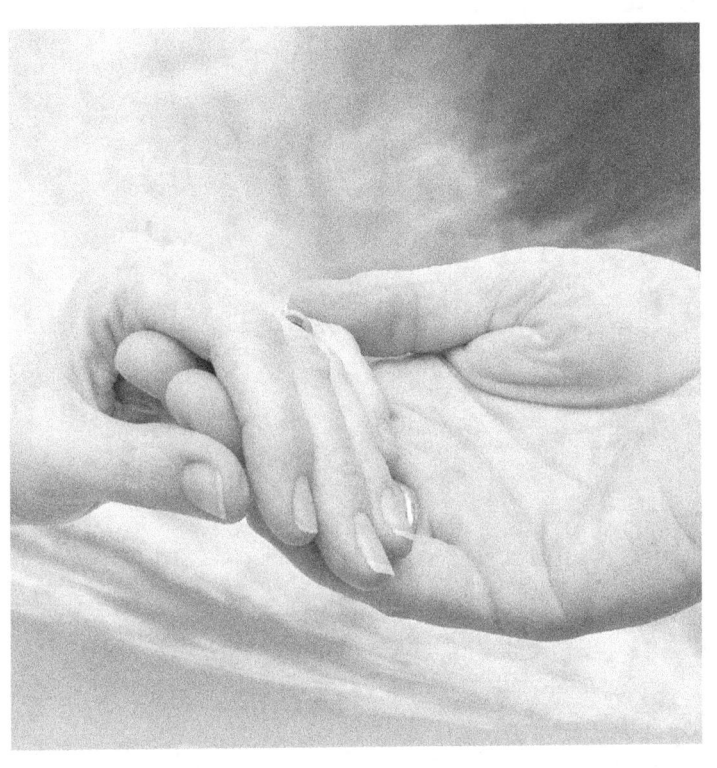

Do not feel shame at being helped

You can't be all things to all people

Don't let anxiety define you,
you still have many other positive qualities

Try not to take on all of someone else's problems

Prolonged bad weather affects even the happiest person

It's not what happens, it's how we respond

Make sure you take a lunch break from work

Your reaction to an event is your choice
and within your control

Simplify your life to achieve balance

Enjoy your own company,
don't be afraid to be alone with your own thoughts

Unhappiness is a selfish act

Change your thoughts and you'll change your mood

Going through difficulties will make you stronger

Take confidence from past successes

Treat yourself fairly as well as others

Help people with their troubles to forget your own

Light candles around your home for a calming atmosphere

Reduce nightmares by recreating the ending in your mind each time you remember one

People who act in spite of their fear are truly brave

Holding on to fears gives them power, let them go

Look forward to something

Quiet contemplation is a good antidote to the
stresses of the day

Don't ruin the present by worrying about the future

Take the future one day at a time,
thinking too far ahead can be overwhelming

www.ingramcontent.com/pod-product-compliance
Lightning Source LLC
Chambersburg PA
CBHW060423290526
45791CB00002B/851